TRIVIA-ON-BOOKS

PRESENTS

Elizabeth Strout's
My Name is Lucy Barton

A TRIVIA GUIDES COLLECTION

Join the trivia club

D1372554

A Letter from Our Editor

To say thank you,

We've included a free gift download of our *All-Time Top 5 Bestselling* Trivia-On-Books yours absolutely free.

To access your free bonus gifts, we're simply asking you to write your review of this purchase and let others know how we did. We're always looking to improve your experience.

Leave My Amazon Review Here

Once you've submitted your review, enter your email for an instant delivery of our *All-Time Top 5 Bestselling* Trivia-On-Books to your inbox.

Enter My Best Email Address Here

What will your triviascore be?

Editors at
Trivia-On-Books

Table of Contents

The First Challenge

Have you read the book?

Question #1

What is the initial reason for Lucy's trip to the hospital?

    a. A check-up

    b. An appendectomy

    c. Chemotherapy

    d. A routine blood test

ANSWER b

An appendectomy

Lucy heads to the hospital for a simple appendectomy. Shortly after the operation, she becomes feverish. Due to a series of complications, Lucy ends up hospitalized in New York City for a total of nine weeks. During this time, she is separated from her family, and loneliness starts to take its toll on her. She wakes up one day, after three weeks of being in the hospital, to find her estranged mother by her bedside.

Question #2

Who asks Lucy's mother to come visit her at the hospital?

    a. Lucy's father

    b. Lucy's sister

    c. Lucy's best friend

    d. Lucy's husband

ANSWER d

Lucy's husband

Since Lucy's hospitalization, her husband has been very busy juggling work and watching over their two daughters. He hasn't had much time to visit her at all. Lucy also mentions her husband never liked hospitals, given his father died in one when he was 14 years old. Lucy's husband one day decides to ask Lucy's mother if she could spend some time at the hospital. He even takes care of the travel expenses for her trip.

Question #3

What is Lucy's occupation?

    a. Writer

    b. Interior designer

    c. Painter

    d. Professor

ANSWER a

Writer

Lucy is a successful writer. In the book, she talks, from the vantage point of the future, about the five nights she spent with her mother during her prolonged hospitalization. She also recalls her complicated childhood and what inspired her to become a professional writer. According to Lucy, the loneliness of her childhood made her want to be a writer. Lucy found solace in reading books, and she thought that writing books would ease the loneliness of others.

Question #4

Who gives Lucy the advice to be a "ruthless writer?"

    a. Jeremy

    b. Larry

    c. Samuel

    d. Teresa

ANSWER a

Jeremy

It is Lucy's friend and neighbor, Jeremy, who tells her to be ruthless in writing. He unfortunately dies of AIDS, but Lucy takes his advice to heart. Lucy knew early on that she wanted to be a writer. Even though she grew up dirt poor, she conquered all odds, went to college, moved to New York City, and strived to be a writer. The success of her writing career, however, strained her relationships with her husband and two daughters.

Question #5

How did Lucy describe her family?

 a. Traditional

  b. Close

  c. Oddities

  d. Broken

ANSWER c

Oddities

Lucy used the word "oddities" to describe her family. They lived in a small rural town in Illinois, in a relative's garage, and were very poor. Growing up, Lucy, her sister, and her brother were often teased by other children. Her father worked on farm machinery and was often fired, while her mother took in sewing. Lucy's father often locked her up in his truck, too, when she misbehaved or a babysitter wasn't available to watch over her.

Question #6

What was Lucy's attitude toward her mother?

    a. Cold

    b. Resentful

    c. Indifferent

    d. Needy

ANSWER d

Needy

Lucy is needy toward her mother. Although she tries to be fine in the story, readers can see that she is desperate for love and affection, especially from her mother. There is some kind of denial on Lucy's part of her mother's capacity for cruelty and abuse. Somehow, it becomes difficult for her to accept that her mother is incapable of addressing her emotional needs. In a way, she remains like a needy child wanting a cold parent's approval.

Question #7

Which character in the book did Lucy consider as a father figure?

    a. Her neighbor

    b. Her doctor

    c. A former professor

    d. A writing mentor

ANSWER b

Her doctor

In *My Name Is Lucy Barton*, Lucy talks about and paints portraits of the different people she loves. Among them is a kind Jewish doctor to whom Lucy says she feels a "deep attachment." She looks at the doctor as a lovely man and a father figure. According to her, the doctor understands her loneliness. Starved for affection as a child, Lucy finds love in the simplest show of kindness from people, the doctor included.

Question #8

What did Lucy and her mother mostly talk about?

    a. A business idea

    b. Current events

    c. Lucy's writing career

d. The life and marriages of people they had both known

ANSWER d

The life and marriages of people they had both known

When Lucy's mother comes to visit her at the hospital, Lucy is surprised. They haven't spoken to each other in years, and now her mother is to stay with her for five days. They mostly talk about the people they both know from Lucy's childhood in Amgash, Illinois. They gossip about people's failed marriages, but these conversations are just on the surface. Readers feel the tension that lies in the unspoken thoughts of the characters.

Question #9

What did Lucy need to hear from her mother?

    a. That she is sorry

    b. That she loves her

    c. That she is going to be more present in her life

    d. That she made many mistakes

ANSWER b

That she loves her

In the story, Lucy is still like a needy child wanting her mother's approval, love, and affection. Despite her troublesome childhood, she still loves her mother, and she hopes she loves her, too. She wants to hear this straight from her mother's mouth. Lucy tries to bring up their issues during her mother's visit to the hospital, but her mother manages to evade these matters and instead initiates gossip about the people they both know.

Question #10

Which author makes an impact on Lucy's Life?

    a. Sarah Payne

    b. Stephen King

    c. Gabriel Garcia Marquez

    d. Elizabeth Strout

ANSWER a

Sarah Payne

Payne is one of the beloved characters that Lucy recalls in the book. She meets the author at one of her workshops, and Payne ends up being a mentor and giving pieces of advice to Lucy. According to Payne, "We only have one story." She also advises Lucy to write without protecting anyone, and she defines writing fiction as reporting "on the human condition to tell us who we are and what we think and what we do."

The Second Challenge

Do you know the author?

A Letter from Our Editor

To say thank you,

We've included a free gift download of our *All-Time Top 5 Bestselling* Trivia-On-Books yours absolutely free.

To access your free bonus gifts, we're simply asking you to write your review of this purchase and let others know how we did. We're always looking to improve your experience.

Leave My Amazon Review Here

Once you've submitted your review, enter your email for an instant delivery of our *All-Time Top 5 Bestselling* Trivia-On-Books to your inbox.

Enter My Best Email Address Here

What will your trivia score be?

Editors at
Trivia-On-Books

Question #1

Which of Elizabeth Strout's novels was made into a television movie?

    a. The Burgess Boys

    b. Amy and Isabelle

    c. Olive Kitteridge

    d. My Name Is Lucy Barton

ANSWER b

Amy and Isabelle

Elizabeth Strout's debut novel titled *Amy and Isabelle* was made into a television movie from Harpo Films, under the "Oprah Winfrey Presents" banner. The television adaptation starred actresses Elisabeth Shue and Hanna Hall as Isabelle and Amy Goodrow, respectively. Strout wrote *Amy and Isabelle* in 1998, and it was published through Random House. The made-for-TV movie aired on ABC on March 4, 2001 and received mixed reviews.

Question #2

Which educational institutions did the author attend?

    a. UCLA and Yale Univerisity

    b. Princeton University and Syracuse University

    c. Bates College and Syracuse University

    d. Brown University and Harvard University

ANSWER c

Bates College and Syracuse University

Elizabeth Strout graduated from Bates College with a degree in English in 1977. After that, she spent a year in Oxford, England. She then went on to study law, and in 1982, she graduated with honors and received her law degree from the Syracuse University College of Law. She then briefly worked for Legal Services before moving to New York City.

Question #3

For which novel did the author receive the Pulitzer Prize for Fiction in

2009?

    a. Abide with Me

    b. The Burgess Boys

    c. My Name Is Lucy Barton

    d. Olive Kitteridge

ANSWER d

Olive Kitteridge

In 2009, Elizabeth Strout was awarded the Pulitzer Prize for Fiction for her novel *Olive Kitteridge*. *Olive Kitteridge*, published in 2008, is the author's third novel. It is a collection of thirteen connected short stories, featuring a title character and a few recurring characters in the coastal town of Crosby, Maine. In 2014, HBO produced a four-part mini series based on the novel. The production was a success, too, winning eight awards at the 2015 Primetime Emmys.

ANSWER a

Cleaning houses

Elizabeth Strout's first ever job was cleaning houses. She was 12 years old then and would visit the houses of elderly women in their small town. The author mentioned in an interview that she actually "hated" the job and would be bored while she did her cleaning duties. According to her, her mind would often wander as she scrubbed kitchen tiles. She would think of other places, like a friend's house or the beach, to escape boredom.

Question #5

What was the author's first job?

    a. Cleaning houses

    b. Waiting tables

    c. Paralegal

    d. Writer's assistant

ANSWER c

During her childhood

Elizabeth Strout knew at a very early age that she had a passion for writing. She was inclined towards writing things down and keeping journals. She loved reading and spent hours in their local library reading fiction books. Her passion for writing continued to her adolescent and adult years. She wrote endlessly and read about the lives of different writers. At age 16, she was already sending out her stories to magazines, and at 26, her first story was published.

Question #4

At which point of the author's life did she realize her love for writing?

    a. During her 20s

    b. Her teenage years

    c. During her childhood

    d. When she turned 30

Question #6

Whom does the author consider as her inspiration for her writing?

    a. Her mother

    b. Her father

    c. Her husband

    d. Her child

ANSWER a

Her mother

Author Elizabeth Strout considers her mother as her inspiration for her writing. In an interview, she talked about how great of a storyteller her mother is. The author, during her younger years, would often listen to her mother as she told stories to her friends. Her mother talked about the lives of others—their families, illnesses, and misfortunes—which made the author realize that the lives of people are the most interesting things to write about.

Question #7

Which book had the greatest influence on the author's writing career?

    a. The Year of Magical Thinking

    b. The Journals of John Cheever

    c. The Unbearable Lightness of Being

    d. One Hundred Years of Solitude

ANSWER b

The Journals of John Cheever

Elizabeth Strout said in an interview that the book *The Journals of John Cheever* had the most influence in her writing career. She had read many books that made an impact on her, but this particular book stood out to her the most. According to her, it was the honestly in Cheever's writing that gave her the courage to continue pursuing writing. She also admires the author's writing skills and ability to eloquently describe his surroundings.

Question #8

What was the author's parents' occupations?

     a. Artists

     b. Lawyers

     c. Doctors

     d. Educators

Answer d

Educators

Elizabeth Strout was born in Portland, Maine and was raised in small towns in Maine and New Hampshire. Both her parents were educators. Her father worked as a science professor, while her mother was a senior school teacher. The author herself was a National Endowment for the Humanities professor at Colgate University, where she lectured about creative writing.

Question #9

Which of the author's books has the same setting as her first novel, *Amy and Isabelle*?

    a. Abide with Me

    b. Olive Kitteridge

    c. My Name Is Lucy Barton

    d. The Burgess Boys

ANSWER d

The Burgess Boys

Elizabeth Strout's fourth book, titled *The Burgess Boys,* has the same setting as her debut novel, *Amy and Isabelle*. The story is set in the fictional town of Shirley Falls. *The Burgess Boys*, published on March 26, 2013 through Random House, follows two brothers, Jim and Bob, who need to return home after their sister Susan's son is accused of a hate crime. They need to use their legal expertise to help their family. Reception for the book has been generally positive.

Question #10

How many novels has the author published?

    a. 6

    b. 8

    c. 5

    d. 3

Elizabeth Strout has released a total of five fiction novels. She started with her debut novel titled *Amy and Isabelle* (1998), which took her six or seven years to write. She then followed it up in 2006 with *Abide with Me*, which got mixed reviews. In 2008, she released her Pulitzer Prize-winning book, *Olive Kitteridge*. In 2013, Strout came out with the well-received family drama, *The Burgess Boys*. Her latest novel is *My Name Is Lucy Barton* (2016).

The Third Challenge

Are you an Avid Fan?

Question #1

When was *My Name is Lucy Barton* released?

a. December 25, 2015

b. July 23, 2015

c. January 12, 2016

d. February 11, 2016

ANSWER c

January 12, 2016

My Name is Lucy Barton, American writer Elizabeth Strout's fifth novel, was first published on January 12, 2016 in the United States through Random House. The book focuses on the complicated relationship between the title character and her mother. It's preceded by *The Burgess Boys*, another title that tackles family issues. *My Name is Lucy Barton* has been positively received by critics, getting praise from both the *AV Club* and the *Washington Post*, to name a few.

Question #2

For which literary prize has the book been longlisted?

    a. Man Booker Prize

    b. Franz Kafka Prize

    c. Nobel Prize in Literature

     d. America Award

ANSWER a

Man Booker Prize

American writer Elizabeth Strout's latest novel, *My Name Is Lucy Barton,* was longlisted in July 2016 for the 2016 Man Booker Prize. The Man Booker Prize, formerly known as the Booker-McConnell Prize, awards every year for the best original novel published in the United Kingdom and is considered a top recognition to be received and usually assures the international success of the winning book and author.

Question #3

For which category was the book listed in the New York Times bestseller list?

    a. Paperback Nonfiction

    b. Hardcover Fiction

    c. Manga

    d. E-book Fiction

ANSWER b

Hardcover Fiction

Elizabeth Strout's fifth novel, *My Name Is Lucy Barton,* is a *New York Times* bestselling book. Shortly after its release on January 12, 2016, it was included in the *New York Times* bestseller list under the Hardcover Fiction category. The January 31, 2016 list also features other bestselling titles such as *The Force Awakens* by Alan Dean Foster, *The Girl on the Train* by Paula Hawkins, and *All the Light We Cannot See* by Anthony Doerr.

Question #4

Which review regarded the book as "deeply affecting?"

    a. The Guardian

    b. Cosmopolitan

    c. Huffington Post

    d. The New York Times

ANSWER a

The Guardian

The Guardian, in a review by writer Hannah Beckman, described Elizabeth Strout's *My Name is Lucy Barton* as a "deeply affecting" piece of writing. The positive review praised Strout's work and its ability to touch the reader, even calling the author a "powerful storyteller." The author is commended for her impeccable writing skills that capture the complexities of human emotions and relationships. According to the review, Strout's latest novel makes for another Pulitzer Prize contender.

Question #5

To which book of the same author is *My Name Is Lucy Barton* often compared?

a. Abide With Me

b. The Burgess Boys

c. Olive Kitteridge

d. Amy and Isabelle

Answer c

Olive Kitteridge

Elizabeth Strout's newest novel, *My Name Is Lucy Barton*, is often compared to her Pulitzer Prize-winning book, *Olive Kitteridge*. Both *The Guardian* and the *New York Times* compared her 2016 book to her 2008 novel. *My Name Is Lucy Barton* focuses on the relationship of Lucy and her mother. *Olive Kitteridge*, on the other hand, features thirteen connected short stories with recurring characters. According to the reviews, the two novels solidify the author's ability to write powerful and moving stories about people and their relationships.

Question #6

Under which type of the fiction genre does the book fall?

    a. Thriller

    b. Romance

    c. Romantic Comedy

    d. Family Life

ANSWER d

Family Life

American writer Elizabeth Strout's *My Name Is Lucy Barton* is considered family life fiction. The author's fifth and latest novel explores the complexity of Lucy and her mother's troubled relationship. It tackles family life and describes the drama around it. This theme is also present in the award-winning writer's other books, *The Burgess Boys*, *Amy and Isabelle*, and *Olive Kitteridge*.

Question #7

For which women's literary prize was the book longlisted?

    a. Baileys Women's Prize for Fiction

    b. The Orange Prize for Fiction

    c. The Women's Prize for Fiction

    d. Women's Fiction Awards

ANSWER a

Baileys Women's Prize for Fiction

Elizabeth Strout's *My Name Is Lucy Barton* was included on the longlist for the Bailey's Women's Prize for Fiction. The longlist was released on March 8, 2016 and includes other titles such as *A God In Ruins* by Kate Atkinson, *The Sacred Chord* by Geraldine Brooks, and more. The Baileys Women's Prize is considered one of the most prestigious award for United Kingdom's women writers.

Question #8

What is the general reception for the book?

a. Mixed

b. Negative

c. Positive

d. None

ANSWER c

Positive

Literary critics have positively received Elizabeth Barton's *My Name Is Lucy*. The author's fifth and latest novel peaked on the *New York Times* bestseller list shortly after its release. Different publications like the *Washington Post*, the *AV Club*, the *New York Times,* and *The Guardian* have released positive reviews for the book and have given praises for the author.

Question #9

Which publication describes the book as "smart and cagey?"

a. Guardian

b. The New York Times

c. Washington Post

d. People

ANSWER c

Washington Post

Writer Lily King, in her review of novelist Elizabeth Strout's *My Name is Lucy Barton* for the *Washington Post*, describes the author's latest novel as "smart and cagey." King praises the book for its wisdom and "solid structure." King also compares Strout to writers Karl Ove Knausgaard and Rachel Cusk; the author marvels at Strout's strong command over the material. This review by the *Washington Post* is just one of the many positive reviews for the book.

Question #10

From which point of view is the book written?

    a. First person

    b. Narrator

    c. Point of view of the mother

    d. Point of view of the husband

ANSWER a

First person

American author Elizabeth Strout's fifth and newest novel, *My Name Is Lucy Barton*, is written in the first person point of view. Lucy, a writer with a troublesome childhood and family life, looks back at the time when she is hospitalized and her estranged mother comes to visit. The first-person voice used in the book is different from the previous use of omniscient narrators in the author's other books like *Olive Kitteridge* and *Amy and Isabelle*.

The Moment of Truth

Results May Vary

Based on the difficulty of the questions you are an Avid Fan if you've received less than "2" wrong.

Last Chance to Download!

GET A BONUS DOWNLOAD OF OUR TOP 5 BESTSELLING TITLES

To say thank you,

We've included a free gift download of our *All-Time Top 5 Bestselling* Trivia-On-Books yours absolutely free.

To access your free bonus gifts, we're simply asking you to write your review of this purchase and let others know how we did. We're always looking to improve your experience.

<u>Leave My Amazon Review Here</u>
Or Choose "Write a Customer Review" on Next Page

Once you've submitted your review, enter your email for an instant delivery of our *All-Time Top 5 Bestselling* Trivia-On-Books to your inbox.

<u>Enter My Best Email Address Here</u>

What will your trivia score be?

Editors at
Trivia-On-Books

Made in the USA
Middletown, DE
04 October 2022

11918041R00040